NO BIG DEAL
BREAD MAKING

MASTER THE ART OF HOMEMADE BREAD

No Big Deal:
Bread Making

A Complete Guide to Homemade Bread: Mastering Artisan Loaves, Sourdough, and Global Bread Recipes for All Skill Levels

Produced by:

David W Crimmins

Copyright © 2024 by David W Crimmins.

All rights reserved. No part of this book may be used or reproduced in any form whatsoever without written permission except in the case of brief quotations in critical articles or reviews.

Printed in the United States of America.

ASIN - ebook: B0DHT476VG

ISBN - Paperback: 9798341329911

ISBN - Hardback: 9798341362192

First Edition: September 2024

Table of Contents

Chapter 1:

Introduction to Bread Making

Bread is one of the most ancient and fundamental foods known to humanity, dating back thousands of years. The aroma of freshly baked bread is enough to warm hearts, spark memories, and fill a home with comfort. However, the idea of making bread from scratch may seem intimidating to some, often viewed as something complicated, time-consuming, or best left to professional bakers. But here's the truth: bread making is no big deal.

In this chapter, we'll explore why baking your own bread is one of the most rewarding activities you can undertake in the kitchen. You'll discover how easy it is to get started with basic techniques, a handful of ingredients, and a bit of patience. Whether you're a complete beginner or someone looking to expand your skills, this book will guide you step by step toward mastering the art of bread making. By the end, you'll realize that, indeed, making bread is no big deal—it's a joy.

1.1 Why Bake Your Own Bread?

In today's world of convenience, it's easy to wonder, *Why bother baking bread when I can just buy a loaf at the store?* While store-bought bread is convenient, it often lacks the depth of flavor, texture, and nutritional benefits that come from a homemade loaf. Here are some compelling reasons why you should consider making your own bread at home:

1. Control Over Ingredients

When you bake bread at home, you control everything that goes into it. There are no preservatives, additives, or excess sugars that are often found in commercial bread. You can opt for organic ingredients, experiment with whole grains, or incorporate seeds and nuts for added nutrition. Whether you're gluten-sensitive or just looking to cut down on processed foods, homemade bread allows you to customize your bread exactly how you like it.

2. Superior Taste and Texture

There's nothing quite like the taste of freshly baked bread. The crispy crust, soft crumb, and complex flavors of homemade bread are hard to beat. When you bake bread at home, you have the opportunity to develop deep flavors through slow fermentation and the careful handling of dough. Whether it's a rustic artisan loaf or a fluffy brioche, the taste of homemade bread far surpasses most store-bought options.

3. A Healthier Option

Not only do you have control over the ingredients, but homemade bread is often healthier. Many store-bought loaves contain processed flours and fillers that strip away the nutrients found in whole grains. When baking at home, you can choose nutrient-dense flours such as whole wheat, rye, or spelt, and avoid the refined sugars and unhealthy fats found in some commercial varieties.

4. The Meditative Process of Bread Making

Bread making is not just about the end product; it's about the process. There is something almost meditative about mixing dough, kneading it by hand, and watching it rise. The slow, rhythmic movements can be deeply satisfying, providing a welcome break from the fast-paced demands of daily life. For many, baking bread becomes a form of mindfulness, an opportunity to slow down and enjoy the simple pleasures of working with one's hands.

5. Cost Savings

Baking your own bread can also be a cost-effective option. While artisanal breads can be expensive when purchased at a bakery, the basic ingredients for bread—flour, water, yeast, and salt—are quite inexpensive. With just a few affordable ingredients, you can produce several loaves at home, saving money in the long run.

1.2 The History of Bread Making

Bread has been a staple in human diets for thousands of years. In fact, bread is one of the oldest prepared foods known to humanity. Early forms of bread date back over 14,000 years to prehistoric societies who ground grains and mixed them with water to form a paste that was cooked on hot stones.

The history of bread is closely tied to the development of agriculture. As humans shifted from nomadic lifestyles to settled farming communities, grains like wheat and barley became essential crops. The discovery of leavening—probably by accident—marked a significant evolution in bread making. Ancient Egyptians are credited with pioneering the use of yeast to leaven bread around 4,000 years ago. This innovation transformed bread from a dense, flat food into the light, airy loaves that we know today.

Over time, different cultures developed their own unique bread-making traditions, using the grains and ingredients available to them. From the unleavened flatbreads of the Middle East to the hearty rye breads of Eastern Europe, bread has taken on a myriad of forms, reflecting both the environment and the values of the people who made it. In many societies, bread became not just a food but a symbol of community and sustenance, integral to religious ceremonies, cultural traditions, and everyday meals.

1.3 Bread Making Around the World

Bread is a global phenomenon, with nearly every culture around the world boasting its own unique bread traditions. While the basic ingredients remain the same, the techniques and styles vary widely depending on regional preferences, climates, and available grains. Let's take a brief look at some iconic bread types from different parts of the world:

1. Sourdough (USA and Europe)

Sourdough, with its tangy flavor and chewy texture, is a favorite in many Western countries. Made by fermenting dough using naturally occurring yeast and lactic acid bacteria, sourdough has a deep, rich flavor and a satisfying texture. It's a staple in countries like France and the United States and has become a symbol of artisanal bread making.

2. Baguette (France)

The French baguette is perhaps one of the most iconic breads in the world. This long, thin loaf is known for its crispy crust and light, airy crumb. Baguettes are a staple in French cuisine, often served with meals or used for sandwiches.

3. Naan (India and Middle East)

Naan is a soft, pillowy flatbread that

originates from India and the Middle East. Traditionally cooked in a tandoor oven, naan is often brushed with butter or ghee and served alongside curries, kebabs, and other dishes.

4. Focaccia (Italy)
Focaccia is a flat, oven-baked Italian bread that is similar to pizza dough. It's usually seasoned with olive oil, herbs, and sometimes topped with vegetables or cheese. Focaccia's fluffy texture and rich flavor make it a popular accompaniment to meals or a delicious snack on its own.

5. Pita (Middle East)
Pita bread, a staple in the Middle East, is a simple flatbread that puffs up during baking to create a pocket. This pocket is perfect for stuffing with ingredients, making pita a versatile bread for sandwiches, dips, and wraps.

Conclusion: Your Bread Making Journey

As we've seen, bread making is a time-honored tradition that transcends cultures and generations. It's an art that has been passed down through families and communities, constantly evolving yet remaining rooted in its simplicity.

With this book, you'll embark on your own bread-making journey. Whether you're trying to recreate the perfect loaf of sourdough or experimenting with new flavors and techniques, the process is as rewarding as the product. By the time you reach the final chapter, you'll have the skills and confidence to bake a variety of delicious breads, from simple everyday loaves to impressive artisanal creations.

So, let's roll up our sleeves, grab some flour, and get started. After all, bread making is no big deal—it's an adventure that begins with just a few simple ingredients.

Chapter 2:

Essential Tools and Ingredients

Before you dive into the world of bread making, it's important to gather the right tools and understand the ingredients that make bread so special. While bread is made from a few simple ingredients, each one plays a vital role in the final product. And while you don't need a fancy kitchen or expensive gadgets to bake great bread, having the right tools will make the process easier and more enjoyable.

In this chapter, we'll cover the essential tools you'll need for bread making, explain the role of key ingredients, and provide tips on choosing the best quality components for your bread.

2.1 Must-Have Tools for Bread Making

One of the best things about bread making is that you don't need a lot of equipment to get started. Unlike some other baking projects, bread is relatively low-tech. However, having a few basic tools on hand will help you create consistent, high-quality loaves and make the process smoother. Here are the essentials:

1. Mixing Bowls

You'll need a few large mixing bowls to prepare your dough. Stainless steel or glass bowls work best because they won't absorb odors or react with acidic ingredients, such as sourdough starter or certain types of yeast. It's helpful to have at least two bowls: one for mixing the dough and another for letting it rise. Make sure the bowls are large enough to accommodate the dough as it doubles in size.

2. A Digital Scale

Precision is key in bread making, and a digital scale is essential for accurately measuring your ingredients. Unlike measuring cups, a scale gives you exact amounts, which is especially important when working with flour. Flour can be compacted or fluffed up, leading to inaccurate measurements when using cups. Weighing your ingredients will give you the most consistent results.

3. A Dough Scraper
Also known as a bench scraper, this tool is incredibly useful for handling dough. A dough scraper helps you divide the dough into portions, shape it on your work surface, and scrape off any sticky dough remnants. It's a versatile, inexpensive tool that will save you a lot of time and effort.

4. A Proofing Basket (Banneton)
If you're planning to make artisan-style bread with a beautiful shape and crust, a proofing basket is a great investment. These baskets are designed to support the dough during its final rise, giving the bread structure and helping it maintain its shape in

the oven. If you don't have a banneton, you can improvise with a bowl lined with a floured kitchen towel.

5. A Kitchen Thermometer

Temperature plays a crucial role in bread making, from the water you use to mix the dough to the internal temperature of your bread as it bakes. A kitchen thermometer helps you ensure that your dough is rising in the right conditions and that your bread is perfectly baked through. For example, yeast is activated best at around 100°F (38°C), and most bread is fully baked when it reaches an internal temperature of 190°F to 210°F (88°C to 99°C).

6. A Dutch Oven (Optional)

If you're interested in making rustic, crusty bread, a Dutch oven can be a game-changer. Baking bread in a Dutch oven traps steam, which helps create that golden, crackly crust that's characteristic of artisan loaves. While not essential, it's a great tool for making bakery-quality bread at home.

7. A Baking Stone or Steel (Optional)

For those looking to replicate a professional bread oven at home, a baking stone or steel is a worthy investment. These heavy slabs are placed in your oven to retain and evenly distribute heat, resulting in better oven spring (the rise of your bread in the oven) and a crisper crust.

2.2 Ingredients Breakdown: Flour, Water, Yeast, and More

At its core, bread is made from just four ingredients: flour, water, yeast, and salt. However, each of these ingredients plays a crucial role in how the bread looks, tastes, and feels. Let's break down each of these components, along with a few optional ingredients that can enhance your bread.

1. Flour

Flour is the backbone of bread, providing structure, flavor, and texture. There are many different types of flour, each with its own properties. Understanding the differences will help you choose the right one for the type of bread you want to bake.

- **All-Purpose Flour**: This is the most commonly used flour and works well for most types of bread. It has a moderate protein content, which makes it versatile for both yeast breads and quick breads.
- **Bread Flour**: Bread flour has a higher protein content (usually around 12-14%) than all-purpose flour, which results in stronger gluten formation. This is ideal for chewy, rustic breads with a strong structure.
- **Whole Wheat Flour**: Made from the entire wheat kernel, whole

wheat flour contains more fiber and nutrients than white flour. It produces a denser loaf with a nutty flavor. Because it absorbs more water, it may require adjustments to hydration levels in your dough.

- **Rye Flour**: Rye flour is often used in combination with wheat flour to produce breads with a distinctive flavor and denser texture. It's less elastic than wheat flour, so it's common to blend the two.
- **Specialty Flours**: Other types of flour, like spelt, einkorn, or gluten-free flours, can also be used in bread making. Each has its own characteristics and requires specific techniques, which we'll explore later in the book.

2. Water

Water hydrates the flour and activates the yeast, but its role goes beyond that. The amount of water you use will determine the dough's consistency, affecting the final texture of your bread. More water leads to a higher hydration dough, which results in a more open crumb (larger air pockets) and a chewier texture. The temperature of the water is also important: warm water helps activate the yeast, while too hot or too cold water can inhibit fermentation.

3. Yeast

Yeast is the magical ingredient that makes bread rise. It's a living organism that feeds on the sugars in the dough, producing carbon dioxide and alcohol. The carbon dioxide gets trapped in the dough, causing it to expand and rise. There are two main types of yeast used in bread making:

- **Active Dry Yeast**: This is the most commonly available yeast. It needs to be dissolved in warm water before being added to the dough.

- **Instant Yeast**: Instant yeast, also called rapid-rise yeast, can be added directly to the dry ingredients without being dissolved first. It's more potent than active dry yeast and works faster.

Some bakers prefer to use natural leavening agents, like sourdough starter, which relies on wild yeast and bacteria to ferment the dough. We'll explore sourdough and other fermentation methods in later chapters.

4. Salt
Salt enhances the flavor of bread and helps control yeast activity. Without salt, bread can taste flat and dull. In addition to flavor, salt also strengthens the gluten network, giving the dough more elasticity and structure.

5. Optional Ingredients
While flour, water, yeast, and salt are

the basics, many breads include additional ingredients to add flavor, texture, or nutritional value.

- **Sugar**: Sugar or honey is often added to sweeten the dough and give the yeast extra food, resulting in a faster rise. Sugar can also help create a darker crust.
- **Fats**: Butter, oil, or eggs can be added to enrich the dough, making it softer and more tender. This is common in brioche, challah, and other enriched breads.
- **Seeds, Nuts, and Grains**: Adding seeds (like sesame, sunflower, or poppy), nuts, or grains (like oats or millet) can add texture, flavor, and nutritional benefits to your bread.
- **Dairy**: Milk or yogurt can add richness and moisture to the dough, making for a softer crumb.

2.3 Choosing the Best Quality Components for Your Bread

When it comes to bread making, the quality of your ingredients can make a significant difference in the flavor and texture of the final product. Here are a few tips for selecting the best ingredients:

- **Flour**: Always use fresh flour. If your flour has been sitting on the shelf for too long, it can go rancid or lose its potency. Consider storing your flour in an airtight container in a cool, dark place or even in the refrigerator for extended freshness.
- **Water**: If your tap water has a strong chlorine taste or other off flavors, it can affect the taste of your bread. If needed, use filtered water for the best results.
- **Yeast**: Check the expiration date on your yeast. Old yeast may not

activate properly, leading to poor rising. Store your yeast in the refrigerator or freezer to extend its shelf life.

By understanding the tools and ingredients involved in bread making, you're now equipped with the knowledge to start baking your first loaf. In the next chapter, we'll explore the fundamental techniques that will help you transform these simple ingredients into delicious, homemade bread. It's time to get hands-on with mixing, kneading, and shaping dough—the core skills that every bread maker should master.

Chapter 3:

The Science of Bread Making

Bread making is often seen as an art, but there's just as much science behind it. Understanding how and why certain processes happen will help you improve your technique, troubleshoot issues, and ultimately become a more confident bread baker. In this chapter, we'll break down the core scientific principles that turn a few simple ingredients—flour, water, yeast, and salt—into a delicious loaf of bread.

3.1 How Yeast Works: The Engine of Bread Rising

At the heart of bread making is fermentation, the process by which yeast converts sugars into carbon dioxide and alcohol. This is what gives bread its rise, its light texture, and its complex flavors.

Yeast as a Living Organism

Yeast is a type of fungus and a living organism. When it's mixed with flour and water, it begins to feed on the sugars naturally present in the flour. Through a process called glycolysis, yeast breaks down these sugars and produces two byproducts: carbon dioxide and alcohol. The carbon dioxide is what causes bread dough to expand and rise, while the alcohol evaporates during baking, contributing to the bread's aroma and flavor.

Types of Yeast

There are several types of yeast used in bread making, and understanding the differences can help you choose the right one for your recipe.

- **Active Dry Yeast**: This yeast is dehydrated and must be dissolved in warm water before use. It has a slower action but produces excellent results.
- **Instant Yeast**: Instant yeast, also known as rapid-rise or bread machine yeast, can be mixed directly into dry ingredients without being dissolved first. It activates faster than active dry yeast.
- **Fresh Yeast**: Fresh or cake yeast is highly perishable and must be kept refrigerated. It's favored by professional bakers for its strong, consistent performance, but it's less commonly used by home bakers due to its short shelf life.

- **Sourdough Starter**: This is a natural form of yeast cultivated over time, made from a mixture of flour and water that captures wild yeast from the air. It requires regular feeding and maintenance, but it produces bread with a unique tangy flavor.

Fermentation and Dough Development

Fermentation is the process that gives bread dough its rise and its flavor. After mixing the dough, the yeast begins to metabolize sugars and release carbon dioxide, causing the dough to expand. As the dough rises, gluten (a network of proteins found in wheat flour) stretches and traps the carbon dioxide, giving the bread structure and a light, airy texture.

Fermentation is also responsible for flavor development. The alcohol and acids produced by yeast during fermentation create complex, rich flavors. This is why dough that ferments for longer periods—such as sourdough—has a deeper, more nuanced taste than bread made with fast-rising yeast.

3.2 The Role of Gluten: The Backbone of Bread

If yeast is the engine of bread rising, gluten is the structure that holds it all together. Gluten is a combination of two proteins found in wheat flour: glutenin and gliadin. When flour is mixed with water, these proteins form a network that gives bread its elasticity, strength, and chew.

Gluten Formation

When you mix flour and water, gluten begins to develop almost immediately. The more you knead the dough, the stronger the gluten network becomes. This is why kneading is so important in bread making—it helps the dough become elastic and gives it the strength needed to trap gas bubbles created by yeast. The result is bread with a light, open crumb and good rise.

However, not all bread needs a strong gluten network. For example, delicate breads like brioche or soft dinner rolls benefit from less gluten development, resulting in a tender, airy texture. This is why enriched doughs, which contain butter or eggs, are often kneaded less vigorously than lean doughs used for crusty breads like baguettes or sourdough.

Gluten and Flour Types
The type of flour you use plays a significant role in gluten development. Flours with higher protein content, such as bread flour, create more gluten and are ideal for breads that require a strong structure, like sandwich loaves or bagels. All-purpose flour has a lower protein content and produces less gluten, making it suitable for softer breads like rolls or flatbreads.

Whole wheat flour contains the bran and germ of the wheat kernel, which can interfere with gluten formation. This is why whole wheat breads tend to be denser and more compact than white breads. To improve the texture of whole wheat bread, many bakers blend whole wheat flour with bread flour to achieve a balance between flavor and structure.

3.3 Fermentation and Proofing: The Two Rises

Once your dough is mixed and kneaded, it's time for fermentation to work its magic. Fermentation happens in two stages: bulk fermentation (the first rise) and proofing (the second rise). Each stage is critical to developing flavor, texture, and volume in your bread.

Bulk Fermentation

During bulk fermentation, the dough undergoes its first rise. This is the stage where yeast ferments the sugars in the dough, producing carbon dioxide and causing the dough to expand. The length of bulk fermentation can vary depending on the recipe, but it's typically between one and two hours at room temperature.

Longer fermentation times—such as an overnight rise in the refrigerator—allow for more complex flavors to develop. The slower fermentation gives the yeast more time to work, resulting in a deeper, richer flavor. This is why some artisanal breads, like sourdough, are left to ferment for many hours or even overnight.

Punching Down the Dough
After the dough has completed its bulk fermentation, you'll often need to "punch down" or degas the dough. This simply means gently pressing down on the dough to release some of the gas that has accumulated. Punching down the dough

redistributes the yeast and sugars, ensuring an even rise during the next stage. It also helps prevent the dough from over-fermenting, which can result in a coarse crumb or flat bread.

Proofing
After the dough has been shaped, it's time for the second rise, or proofing. Proofing allows the dough to relax and expand further, giving the bread its final volume and shape. The proofing time varies depending on the type of bread and the temperature of your kitchen, but it generally lasts between 30 minutes and two hours.

One way to check if your dough is properly proofed is to gently press your finger into the surface of the dough. If the indentation springs back slowly, the dough is ready to bake. If it springs back too quickly, the dough may need more time. If it doesn't spring back at all, the dough may be over-proofed, which can lead to flat or collapsed bread.

3.4 Baking: Heat, Oven Spring, and the Maillard Reaction

The final stage of bread making is baking, where all the scientific processes come together to transform your dough into a loaf of bread. The heat of the oven activates the remaining yeast, causes the dough to expand rapidly, and forms the crust.

Oven Spring

The first few minutes of baking are crucial for bread development. This is when "oven spring" occurs—the rapid rise of the dough as the heat causes the remaining yeast to produce one final burst of carbon dioxide. At the same time, the water in the dough turns into steam, causing the dough to expand. The heat also sets the gluten structure, locking in the bread's final shape.

Steam and Crust Formation

Steam is essential for creating a good

crust. It keeps the surface of the dough moist during the first part of baking, allowing the dough to expand without drying out. This is why many bakers use methods to introduce steam into the oven, such as baking bread in a covered Dutch oven or placing a pan of water in the oven during baking. Once the dough has expanded, the moisture evaporates, allowing the crust to form.

The Maillard Reaction
The Maillard reaction is a chemical process that occurs when amino acids and sugars in the dough react at high temperatures, producing the golden-brown color and complex flavors we associate with freshly baked bread. This is what gives bread its irresistible crust and toasty aroma.

To maximize the Maillard reaction, many bakers raise the oven temperature for the first 10–15 minutes of baking, then lower it for the remainder of the time. This creates a crisp, caramelized crust while ensuring the interior of the bread bakes through evenly.

Conclusion: Mastering the Science Behind Bread Making

Now that you understand the science of bread making—how yeast ferments dough, the importance of gluten, the process of fermentation and proofing, and the final baking stages—you can apply this knowledge to improve your baking skills. By recognizing how these scientific principles work, you'll be able to adjust your techniques, troubleshoot issues, and create consistently delicious bread.

In the next chapter, we'll move from the science to the practical side, covering the basic techniques of mixing, kneading, and shaping dough. These are the hands-on skills that every baker needs to master, and by the end of the chapter, you'll be ready

to bake your first loaf of bread with
confidence.

Chapter 4:

Basic Bread Making Techniques

Now that you understand the science behind bread making, it's time to dive into the hands-on process. The journey from simple ingredients to a freshly baked loaf of bread begins with mastering the core techniques: mixing, kneading, proofing, and shaping. These fundamental skills are the building blocks of bread making, and once you're comfortable with them, you'll be able to bake a wide variety of breads with confidence.

In this chapter, we'll guide you through each of these basic techniques step-by-step. We'll also cover some common variations and tips to help you refine your skills. By the end of this chapter, you'll be ready to bake your first loaf of bread using these essential methods.

4.1 Mixing the Dough: Bringing Ingredients Together

Mixing is the first step in bread making, and it's where the magic starts. While it may seem like a simple process, how you mix your ingredients can have a significant impact on the texture and structure of your bread.

The Initial Mix

To begin, combine your flour, water, yeast, and salt in a large mixing bowl. If you're using active dry yeast, dissolve it in warm water first to activate it. For instant yeast, you can mix it directly with the dry ingredients. Many bread recipes also call for a small amount of sugar or honey to feed the yeast and speed up the fermentation process.

Start by stirring the ingredients together with a wooden spoon or spatula until they form a rough dough. At this stage, the goal is to ensure that all the flour is hydrated and that the ingredients are evenly distributed. If the dough feels too dry or too sticky, you can adjust by adding a bit more water or flour as needed. The dough should come together into a shaggy mass, and while it might look messy, that's perfectly fine.

Autolyse: A Rest Before Kneading
For certain types of bread, such as rustic or artisan loaves, an autolyse phase can improve the final texture. Autolyse is simply a short resting period after the initial mixing, where the flour is allowed to absorb the water fully before kneading begins. This rest, usually 20 to 30 minutes, allows the gluten to start developing on its own, which can make the dough easier to handle and give the final bread a better crumb structure.

4.2 Kneading the Dough: Developing Gluten

Kneading is one of the most important skills to master in bread making. This is where you strengthen the dough by developing the gluten network, which gives your bread structure and elasticity. Without proper kneading, your bread might end up dense and heavy rather than light and airy.

How to Knead by Hand
Start by turning the dough out onto a lightly floured surface. To knead, press the heel of your hand into the dough, pushing it away from you. Then fold the dough over itself, give it a quarter turn, and repeat the process. As you continue to knead, the dough will become smoother and more elastic. The goal is to stretch and fold the dough repeatedly to build up the gluten structure.

Kneading typically takes around 8 to 10 minutes by hand. You'll know the dough is ready when it's soft, stretchy, and smooth. If you poke it with your finger, it should spring back slightly.

Another test is the "windowpane test": gently stretch a small piece of dough between your fingers—if it forms a thin, translucent membrane without tearing, your gluten is fully developed.

Using a Stand Mixer

If you have a stand mixer, kneading can be done with the dough hook attachment. Mix the dough on low speed for about 5 to 7 minutes, or until it becomes smooth and elastic. Keep in mind that a mixer will develop gluten faster than kneading by hand, so be careful not to overwork the dough.

Common Kneading Mistakes

One common mistake is adding too much flour during kneading. It's tempting to sprinkle extra flour when the dough feels sticky, but too much flour can result in a dry, tough loaf. Instead, use just enough flour to keep the dough from sticking to your hands and work surface. As you knead, the dough will naturally become less sticky as the gluten develops.

Another mistake is under-kneading, which can leave you with a dense, poorly risen loaf. Be patient and trust the process—proper kneading is essential for creating a strong dough that will rise well and have a good texture.

4.3 Proofing: The First Rise

Once the dough has been kneaded, it's time to let it rest and rise, allowing the yeast to do its work. This stage is known as proofing or the first rise, and it's where the dough will expand significantly as the yeast ferments and produces carbon dioxide.

How to Proof Dough
Place your kneaded dough in a lightly greased bowl, cover it with a clean kitchen towel or plastic wrap, and leave it to rise in a warm, draft-free

place. The ideal temperature for proofing is around 75°F to 80°F (24°C to 27°C). A cold kitchen will slow down fermentation, while a hot environment can overactivate the yeast, causing the dough to overproof.

Proofing times vary depending on the recipe, but generally, the dough should rise for about 1 to 2 hours or until it has doubled in size. If you're unsure whether your dough has proofed enough, press two fingers lightly into the surface—if the indentation remains, your dough is ready for the next step.

Slow Fermentation: The Refrigerator Method

Some recipes call for slow fermentation, where the dough rises in the refrigerator over several hours or even overnight. This method allows for more complex flavor development as the yeast works more slowly in a cold environment. Slow fermentation is often used for artisan breads like sourdough, and it results in a more flavorful loaf with a chewy texture.

4.4 Shaping the Dough: Forming Your Loaf

Once your dough has completed its first rise, it's time to shape it into its final form. Shaping is more than just making the dough look nice—it also helps create structure and tension on the surface, which contributes to a good rise and a pleasing crumb in the finished bread.

Punching Down the Dough

Before shaping, you'll need to "punch down" the dough to release some of the built-up gas from fermentation. This isn't as aggressive as it sounds— simply press down on the dough gently to deflate it slightly. This step helps redistribute the yeast and creates a more uniform rise during the second proofing.

Basic Shaping Techniques

The exact method for shaping depends on the type of bread you're making. Here are a few common techniques:

- **Boules and Rounds**: For round loaves like boules, gently stretch and fold the edges of the dough toward the center, creating surface tension on the outside. Then flip the dough over so the smooth side is on top, and gently rotate the dough, tucking the edges under as you go to create a tight, round shape.
- **Loaves**: For sandwich loaves, press the dough into a rectangle, fold the shorter edges in toward the center, and roll the dough into a tight log. Place the log seam-side down in a greased loaf pan, and it will rise into the familiar rectangular shape.
- **Batards and Baguettes**: For elongated loaves like batards or baguettes, shape the dough into

a rectangle, then fold it in thirds lengthwise. Seal the edges with your fingers, and gently roll the dough back and forth to create a long, narrow shape.

Creating Surface Tension

When shaping dough, it's important to create tension on the surface. This helps the dough hold its shape during the second rise and baking. To do this, stretch the surface of the dough gently as you shape it, tucking any seams or folds underneath. A smooth, taut surface will also encourage a good oven spring, resulting in a loaf with a nice rise and an attractive crust.

4.5 The Second Proof: Final Rise Before Baking

After shaping, the dough needs to undergo a second proof, allowing it to rise again and develop its final volume. This is typically a shorter rise than the first proof, lasting anywhere

from 30 minutes to 2 hours,
depending on the recipe and the
temperature of your kitchen.

How to Know When Your Dough is Ready to Bake

To check if your dough is ready for the
oven, use the "poke test": gently
press your finger into the dough—if
the indentation springs back slowly,
the dough is fully proofed. If it springs
back too quickly, it needs more time.
If it doesn't spring back at all, the
dough may be overproofed, which
could lead to a flatter, less impressive
loaf.

4.6 Scoring and Baking

Once your dough is fully proofed, it's
time to bake! Before placing your loaf
in the oven, you'll need to score the
top with a sharp knife or a bread
lame. Scoring creates intentional weak
points in the dough, allowing it to

expand properly in the oven without tearing. For round loaves, a simple cross or a few diagonal slashes work well. For baguettes, several horizontal slashes down the length of the loaf will do the trick.

After scoring, transfer the dough to a preheated oven and bake according to your recipe's instructions. Most bread recipes call for baking at a high temperature, around 450°F (230°C), to create a crisp crust and encourage oven spring.

Conclusion: Building Confidence with Basic Techniques

Now that you've learned the core techniques of mixing, kneading, proofing, shaping, and baking, you're well on your way to becoming a confident bread baker. These steps may seem simple, but they are the foundation of every great loaf. In the next chapter, we'll explore simple bread recipes that you can use to put these techniques into practice, starting with a classic white loaf and moving on to more complex variations.

Chapter 5:

Simple Bread Recipes

Now that you've mastered the essential techniques of bread making, it's time to put them into practice with some simple bread recipes. These recipes are perfect for beginners and serve as the foundation for more advanced bread baking as you grow more confident. From a basic white loaf to a rustic artisan bread, these straightforward recipes will allow you to explore different flavors and textures, all while reinforcing your understanding of dough handling, proofing, and baking.

This chapter will cover five easy-to-follow bread recipes: basic white bread, whole wheat bread, no-knead bread, rustic artisan bread, and focaccia. Each recipe will include step-by-step instructions to ensure your success.

5.1 Basic White Bread

A classic loaf of white bread is a staple in many households. It's soft, tender, and perfect for sandwiches or toast. This simple recipe will teach you how to make a reliable loaf of white bread with minimal ingredients and effort.

Ingredients

- 4 cups all-purpose flour
- 2 ¼ tsp (1 packet) active dry yeast
- 1 ½ tsp salt
- 2 tbsp sugar
- 1 ½ cups warm water (about 110°F/45°C)
- 2 tbsp unsalted butter, melted

Instructions

1. **Activate the Yeast**: In a small bowl, combine the warm water and sugar, then stir in the yeast. Let it sit for 5 to 10 minutes until the yeast becomes foamy.

2. **Mix the Dough**: In a large mixing bowl, combine the flour and salt. Pour the yeast mixture into the bowl, followed by the melted butter. Stir with a wooden spoon until the dough comes together into a shaggy mass.
3. **Knead the Dough**: Transfer the dough to a lightly floured surface and knead for about 8 to 10 minutes until it becomes smooth and elastic. If the dough is too sticky, add a little more flour, one tablespoon at a time.
4. **First Rise**: Place the kneaded dough in a lightly greased bowl, cover with a kitchen towel, and let it rise in a warm place for about 1 to 1 ½ hours, or until it has doubled in size.
5. **Shape the Dough**: After the dough has risen, punch it down to release the gas, then shape it into a loaf. Place the dough in a greased 9x5-inch loaf pan, cover, and let it rise again for 30 to 45

minutes, or until the dough rises just above the edge of the pan.

6. **Bake the Bread**: Preheat your oven to 375°F (190°C). Once the dough has completed its second rise, bake for 30 to 35 minutes, or until the top is golden brown and the loaf sounds hollow when tapped. Remove the bread from the pan and cool on a wire rack before slicing.

5.2 Whole Wheat Bread

Whole wheat bread is a healthier alternative to white bread, as it's made from the entire wheat kernel, providing more fiber, vitamins, and minerals. This recipe balances the nuttiness of whole wheat flour with a soft, moist texture.

Ingredients

- 3 cups whole wheat flour

- 1 ½ cups bread flour (or all-purpose flour)
- 2 ¼ tsp (1 packet) active dry yeast
- 1 ½ tsp salt
- 2 tbsp honey or sugar
- 1 ½ cups warm water (about 110°F/45°C)
- 2 tbsp vegetable oil

Instructions

1. **Activate the Yeast**: In a small bowl, combine the warm water, honey (or sugar), and yeast. Let it sit for 5 to 10 minutes until the yeast becomes foamy.
2. **Mix the Dough**: In a large mixing bowl, combine the whole wheat flour, bread flour, and salt. Add the yeast mixture and vegetable oil. Stir with a wooden spoon until a dough forms.
3. **Knead the Dough**: Transfer the dough to a floured surface and knead for 10 to 12 minutes, adding a little more flour if

needed. Whole wheat dough tends to be denser, so it may require more time to become smooth and elastic.

4. **First Rise**: Place the dough in a greased bowl, cover, and let it rise in a warm place for 1 to 1 ½ hours, or until doubled in size.

5. **Shape the Dough**: After the first rise, punch the dough down and shape it into a loaf. Place it in a greased loaf pan, cover, and let it rise for another 30 to 45 minutes.

6. **Bake the Bread**: Preheat your oven to 375°F (190°C). Bake for 35 to 40 minutes, or until the top is golden and the loaf sounds hollow when tapped. Cool on a wire rack before slicing.

5.3 No-Knead Bread

No-knead bread is the perfect recipe for those who want to make homemade bread with minimal effort. The long fermentation process does the work of kneading for you, resulting in a rustic, crusty loaf with an open crumb.

Ingredients

- 3 cups all-purpose flour
- ¼ tsp instant yeast
- 1 ½ tsp salt
- 1 ½ cups warm water

Instructions

1. **Mix the Dough**: In a large bowl, combine the flour, yeast, and salt. Add the warm water and stir until a sticky dough forms. The dough will look shaggy and wet, but that's normal for no-knead bread.
2. **First Rise**: Cover the bowl with plastic wrap or a kitchen towel and let the dough rise at room temperature for 12 to 18 hours. The dough should double in size

and have a bubbly, sticky surface.

3. **Shape the Dough**: After the first rise, turn the dough out onto a well-floured surface and shape it into a rough ball. Place the dough seam-side down on a piece of parchment paper and let it rest for 30 minutes while you preheat the oven.

4. **Preheat the Oven and Dutch Oven**: Place a Dutch oven (or heavy pot with a lid) in the oven and preheat to 450°F (230°C) for 30 minutes.

5. **Bake the Bread**: Carefully lift the dough on the parchment paper and place it in the hot Dutch oven. Cover with the lid and bake for 30 minutes. Remove the lid and bake for another 10 to 15 minutes, until the crust is deep golden brown. Let the bread cool on a wire rack before slicing.

5.4 Rustic Artisan Bread

Artisan bread is known for its chewy crust, open crumb, and deep flavor. This recipe uses a longer fermentation to develop complex flavors and a beautiful crust.

Ingredients

- 4 cups bread flour
- 2 tsp salt
- 1 tsp instant yeast
- 1 ½ cups water, at room temperature

Instructions

1. **Mix the Dough**: In a large bowl, combine the flour, yeast, and salt. Add the water and stir until a sticky dough forms. Cover the bowl with a kitchen towel and let it rest for 15 to 20 minutes to allow the flour to fully hydrate.

2. **Knead and First Rise**: Turn the dough out onto a floured surface and knead for about 5 minutes until smooth and elastic. Place the dough in a greased bowl, cover, and let it rise for 1 ½ to 2 hours, or until doubled in size.
3. **Shape and Proof the Dough**: Turn the dough out onto a lightly floured surface, gently stretch it into a rectangle, and fold it in thirds. Shape it into a round boule or an oval batard, then place it seam-side down in a proofing basket or bowl. Let it rise for another 30 to 60 minutes.
4. **Preheat the Oven**: Preheat your oven to 450°F (230°C), placing a baking stone or steel inside to heat up, and a pan of water on the lower rack to create steam.
5. **Bake the Bread**: Turn the dough out onto a baking sheet or directly onto the preheated stone. Score the top with a sharp

knife and bake for 30 to 40 minutes, until the crust is golden brown and the bread sounds hollow when tapped. Cool on a wire rack before slicing.

5.5 Focaccia

Focaccia is an Italian flatbread that's easy to make and full of flavor. It's great as a snack, side dish, or even used as sandwich bread. The olive oil and herbs give it a rich, aromatic taste.

Ingredients

- 4 cups all-purpose flour
- 2 ¼ tsp (1 packet) active dry yeast
- 1 ½ cups warm water
- 1 tsp salt
- ¼ cup olive oil (plus more for drizzling)
- Fresh rosemary, sea salt, and garlic (optional, for topping)

Instructions

1. **Activate the Yeast**: In a bowl, combine the warm water and yeast. Let it sit for 5 minutes until foamy.
2. **Mix the Dough**: In a large bowl, mix the flour and salt. Add the yeast mixture and olive oil. Stir until the dough comes together, then knead for 5 to 7 minutes until smooth.
3. **First Rise**: Place the dough in an oiled bowl, cover, and let it rise for about 1 hour, or until doubled in size.
4. **Shape the Dough**: Punch down the dough and press it into a greased baking sheet. Use your fingers to dimple the surface of the dough. Drizzle with olive oil and sprinkle with sea salt, rosemary, and garlic, if desired.
5. **Bake**: Preheat your oven to 400°F (200°C) and bake the focaccia for 20 to 25 minutes, or

until golden brown. Let it cool
before slicing.

Conclusion: Mastering Simple Bread Recipes

These five simple bread recipes will
help you build your skills and
confidence in the kitchen. Whether
you're baking a soft white loaf or a
rustic artisan bread, these recipes
offer a great starting point for home
bakers. In the next chapter, we'll
explore more advanced bread-making
techniques and recipes, allowing you
to take your baking to the next level.

Chapter 6:

Sourdough and Fermented Breads

Sourdough bread has made a remarkable resurgence in recent years, celebrated for its complex flavor, chewy texture, and wholesome qualities. Beyond just being a trend, sourdough baking represents one of the oldest and most traditional methods of bread making, relying on wild yeast and lactic acid bacteria for fermentation. Unlike bread made with commercial yeast, sourdough has a unique, slightly tangy flavor profile and is often easier to digest.

In this chapter, we'll dive into the fascinating world of sourdough and other fermented breads. You'll learn how to create and maintain a sourdough starter, understand the benefits of fermentation, and explore the step-by-step process for baking your first loaf of sourdough. We'll also cover some other fermented bread options, such as rye bread and flatbreads, which use different techniques to achieve their distinctive flavors.

6.1 Creating and Maintaining a Sourdough Starter

A sourdough starter is a live culture made from flour and water that contains naturally occurring yeast and bacteria. Unlike commercial yeast, which provides quick and reliable leavening, sourdough starter relies on the slow fermentation of wild yeast, which is found on the surface of grains and in the air around us. Developing a sourdough starter is a process that takes patience, but once it's active, it can be kept alive and used for years.

Starting Your Sourdough Culture
Creating a sourdough starter from scratch is simple, but it requires a bit of attention each day during the first week. You'll need only two ingredients: flour and water.

Ingredients

- 1 cup whole wheat flour (or all-purpose flour)
- 1 cup water (filtered, room temperature)

Day 1: Starting the Culture

1. Mix 1 cup of whole wheat flour and 1 cup of water in a clean, non-reactive container (glass or plastic works best).
2. Stir vigorously until the mixture is smooth. Cover loosely with a lid or cloth to allow airflow, and let it sit at room temperature (70°F to 75°F) for 24 hours.

Day 2: Feeding the Starter

1. After 24 hours, you may see some bubbles forming, indicating that fermentation has begun. Discard half of the mixture (you can throw it away or compost it) and add 1 cup of flour and ½ cup of water to the remaining starter. Stir well and cover loosely again.
2. Leave the mixture at room temperature for another 24 hours.

Days 3-7: Continue Feeding

1. Repeat the feeding process every 24 hours, discarding half of the starter each time and replenishing it with fresh flour and water. By days 4 or 5, the starter should begin to rise and fall, become bubbly, and have a tangy smell. This is a sign that the wild yeast and bacteria are becoming active.
2. By day 7, your starter should be ready to use in baking. It should have a pleasant sour aroma, be bubbly, and double in size within a few hours after feeding.

Maintaining Your Sourdough Starter

Once your starter is active, you can either continue feeding it daily if you plan to bake often, or store it in the refrigerator. If refrigerated, feed the starter once a week by discarding half and replenishing it with fresh flour and water. When you're ready to bake, remove the starter from the fridge, feed it, and allow it to come to room temperature before using it in a recipe.

6.2 Making Classic Sourdough Bread

Sourdough bread has a rustic charm and a deeply satisfying flavor that comes from the slow fermentation process. It has a chewy texture, crisp crust, and slightly tangy taste. While making sourdough requires some time and patience, the actual process is relatively simple once you've mastered the basic techniques. Below is a classic sourdough recipe that will yield one large loaf or two smaller ones.

Ingredients

- 500g bread flour (about 4 cups)
- 100g active sourdough starter (about ½ cup)
- 350g water (about 1 ½ cups)
- 10g salt (about 1 ½ tsp)

Instructions

1. **Mix the Dough**
   In a large mixing bowl, combine the flour and water. Stir with a wooden spoon or your hands until all the flour is hydrated. Cover the bowl with a kitchen towel and let it rest for 30 minutes—this rest period is known as autolyse and allows the flour to absorb the water, making the dough easier to work with.

2. **Add the Starter and Salt**
   After the autolyse, add the active sourdough starter and salt to the dough. Mix the ingredients together by folding and gently stretching the dough with your hands. The dough will feel sticky, but as you work it, it will become more elastic. Cover the bowl again and let the dough rest for 30 minutes.

3. **Bulk Fermentation and Stretch & Fold**

Over the next 3 to 4 hours, allow the dough to ferment at room temperature. During this time, you'll perform a series of "stretch and fold" techniques to strengthen the gluten network. Every 30 minutes, gently lift one side of the dough, stretch it upward, and fold it over itself. Rotate the bowl 90 degrees and repeat until all sides have been stretched and folded. Cover the dough after each set of folds.

4. **Shaping the Dough**

Once the dough has risen and looks bubbly and light, it's time to shape it. Turn the dough out onto a lightly floured surface and gently shape it into a round (boule) or oval (batard) shape. Place the shaped dough in a proofing basket or a bowl lined with a floured kitchen towel. Cover it and let it rest for 1 to 2 hours, or refrigerate overnight for an even longer fermentation.

5. **Preheat the Oven and Dutch Oven**
   If you're using a Dutch oven to bake your sourdough, place it in the oven and preheat to 450°F (230°C). Let the Dutch oven heat up for at least 30 minutes.
6. **Bake the Sourdough**
   Carefully remove the hot Dutch oven from the oven and gently transfer the proofed dough (still on its parchment paper) into the pot. Score the top of the dough with a sharp knife or bread lame to allow it to expand while baking. Cover with the lid and bake for 20 minutes.
   After 20 minutes, remove the lid and bake for another 20 to 25 minutes, or until the crust is deep golden brown. The bread should sound hollow when tapped on the bottom. Remove the loaf from the Dutch oven and cool on a wire rack before slicing.

6.3 Fermented Breads: Rye and Other Variants

While sourdough is one of the most popular types of fermented bread, there are many other varieties that rely on fermentation to achieve their distinctive flavors. Rye bread, in particular, uses a fermentation process that yields a hearty, dense loaf with a slightly sour taste. Here's a look at how to make a basic fermented rye bread and some other fermented bread options.

Rye Bread

Rye bread is made using rye flour, which has less gluten than wheat flour. As a result, rye bread tends to be denser and moister than other types of bread. The fermentation process in rye bread, often enhanced with a sourdough starter, gives it its signature flavor.

Ingredients

- 300g rye flour (about 2 ½ cups)
- 200g bread flour (about 1 ½ cups)
- 100g sourdough starter (about ½ cup)
- 350g water (about 1 ½ cups)
- 10g salt (about 1 ½ tsp)
- 1 tbsp caraway seeds (optional, for flavor)

Instructions

1. **Mix the Dough**
   Combine the rye flour, bread flour, water, sourdough starter, and salt in a large mixing bowl. Stir until a sticky dough forms. Rye dough will be stickier than wheat dough due to its lower gluten content, so don't worry if it feels different.
2. **Bulk Fermentation**
   Cover the dough and let it rise at room temperature for 3 to 4 hours, or until it has visibly puffed up. You can perform a few gentle stretch-and-folds during

this time to help strengthen the dough.

3. **Shape and Proof**
Turn the dough out onto a floured surface and shape it into a round or oval loaf. Place the shaped dough in a proofing basket and let it rise for another 1 to 2 hours.

4. **Bake the Rye Bread**
Preheat your oven to 450°F (230°C) and bake the rye bread for 40 to 45 minutes, or until it's dark brown and firm. Let the bread cool completely before slicing.

6.4 The Health Benefits of Fermented Breads

Fermented breads, particularly sourdough, are known for being easier to digest than their non-fermented counterparts. The slow fermentation process breaks down gluten and phytic acid, both of which can cause digestive issues for some people. Additionally, the lactic acid bacteria in sourdough improve the absorption of minerals like magnesium, calcium, and zinc, making these breads more nutritious.

Conclusion: The Art of Fermented Bread Making

Sourdough and other fermented breads represent a deeply satisfying way to engage with traditional bread making. While they require a little more patience than quick-rise breads, the rewards are immense—rich flavors, chewy textures, and health benefits that are hard to beat. With the recipes and techniques in this chapter, you're well on your way to mastering the art of sourdough and fermented bread making.

In the next chapter, we'll delve into advanced bread-making techniques, including shaping more complex loaves, incorporating add-ins, and using specialized baking tools to elevate your bread to the next level.

Chapter 7:

Advanced Bread Making Techniques

At this stage in your bread-making journey, you've already learned the basics of mixing, kneading, proofing, and baking. You've explored simple recipes and have a firm grasp on sourdough and fermented breads.

Now, it's time to elevate your skills with more advanced bread-making techniques. In this chapter, we'll dive into sophisticated methods such as high-hydration dough handling, advanced shaping techniques, lamination, and enriching doughs. We'll also explore how to incorporate add-ins like herbs, nuts, seeds, and fruits, as well as the nuances of aging and brining to craft complex flavors.

By mastering these advanced techniques, you'll gain more control over your dough, allowing you to create artisanal breads with professional quality, flavor, and texture.

7.1 Understanding High-Hydration Doughs

High-hydration doughs are breads that use a higher ratio of water to flour, typically 75% hydration or more. These doughs can be challenging to work with due to their sticky nature, but the rewards are worth the effort. High-hydration doughs produce loaves with a more open crumb (large, irregular holes), a chewy texture, and a crispy crust. Classic examples include ciabatta and some styles of sourdough.

The Challenges of High-Hydration Doughs

Handling high-hydration dough requires a gentler touch than traditional lower-hydration doughs. These doughs tend to be wetter and stickier, making them difficult to knead and shape. However, the key to working with high-hydration dough is learning how to handle the dough properly, using techniques such as the "stretch and fold" method, which replaces kneading and strengthens the dough's gluten network.

Techniques for High-Hydration Doughs

1. **Mixing**: High-hydration doughs don't need vigorous kneading. Instead, after the initial mix, let the dough rest (autolyse) for 20-30 minutes. This allows the flour to hydrate and gluten to form naturally, making the dough easier to handle.
2. **Stretch and Fold**: Rather than traditional kneading, stretch-and-fold techniques work best for high-hydration doughs. Every 30 minutes during the bulk fermentation process, gently lift one side of the dough, stretch it upward, and fold it over itself. Repeat on all four sides. This strengthens the gluten network without overworking the dough, helping it maintain its structure while allowing it to develop large air pockets.
3. **Shaping**: Because of the dough's wetness, shaping can be tricky. Use well-floured hands and work on a generously floured surface.

Avoid overhandling the dough to preserve the air pockets and achieve the desired open crumb.

4. **Baking**: High-hydration breads benefit from being baked in a hot, steamy environment, which helps create a crisp crust. A Dutch oven works well for this, or you can add a pan of water to your oven to generate steam during the first 10 to 15 minutes of baking.

7.2 Laminating Dough: Croissants and Puff Pastry

Lamination is a technique used to create layers in dough by incorporating butter and folding the dough repeatedly. It's the method behind flaky, buttery pastries like croissants and puff pastry. While lamination requires precision and time, the results are impressive—each bite reveals delicate, crispy layers that melt in your mouth.

The Process of Laminating Dough

The goal of lamination is to create multiple thin layers of dough and butter, which will expand and separate during baking, producing a flaky texture. The basic process involves rolling out the dough, placing butter on top, and folding the dough over itself several times, with chilling in between.

Ingredients for Laminated Dough (Croissants)

- 500g all-purpose flour (about 4 cups)
- 10g salt (about 1 ½ tsp)
- 50g sugar (about ¼ cup)
- 10g instant yeast (about 2 ¼ tsp)
- 300g water or milk (about 1 ¼ cups)
- 250g unsalted butter (for lamination)

Instructions for Laminating Dough

1. **Prepare the Dough**: Mix the flour, salt, sugar, yeast, and water (or milk) in a bowl until a soft dough forms. Knead the dough briefly until smooth, then shape it into a rectangle. Wrap the dough in plastic and chill for at least 30 minutes to firm up.

2. **Prepare the Butter Block**: While the dough is chilling, prepare the butter for lamination. Cut the butter into slices and place them between two sheets of parchment paper. Use a rolling pin to gently pound and shape the butter into a thin, flat rectangle about half the size of the dough. Chill the butter until firm but pliable.

3. **Laminate the Dough**: Roll out the dough into a rectangle that's about twice the size of the butter block. Place the butter in the center of the dough and fold the

dough over the butter, sealing the edges to encase the butter completely.

4. **Rolling and Folding (Turns)**: Roll the dough out again into a long rectangle, then fold it into thirds, like folding a letter. This is called a "turn." Chill the dough for 30 minutes, then repeat the process two more times. Each turn creates more layers of butter and dough. After the final turn, chill the dough for at least an hour before shaping.

5. **Shaping Croissants**: Roll the laminated dough into a large rectangle and cut it into triangles. Roll each triangle from the wide end to the point to form a croissant shape. Let the croissants proof at room temperature until they puff up, about 1 to 2 hours.

6. **Baking**: Preheat the oven to 400°F (200°C). Brush the croissants with an egg wash and

bake for 15 to 20 minutes, or until golden brown and crispy.

7.3 Enriched Doughs: Brioche, Challah, and Sweet Breads

Enriched doughs differ from lean doughs because they contain added fats, sugar, eggs, or dairy, which give the bread a rich flavor and tender crumb. Common examples of enriched doughs include brioche, challah, and sweet breads like cinnamon rolls. These doughs are typically softer and more luxurious than traditional breads, making them perfect for special occasions.

Ingredients for Enriched Doughs
Enriched dough recipes often include:

- **Butter or Oil**: Adds richness and moisture to the dough.
- **Eggs**: Contribute to the dough's structure, flavor, and color.

- **Milk**: Provides additional moisture and a tender texture.
- **Sugar**: Feeds the yeast, enhances browning, and sweetens the dough.

Brioche Recipe
Brioche is a classic example of enriched dough, known for its buttery richness and soft texture.

Ingredients

- 500g bread flour (about 4 cups)
- 50g sugar (about ¼ cup)
- 10g salt (about 1 ½ tsp)
- 10g instant yeast (about 2 ¼ tsp)
- 5 large eggs
- 250g unsalted butter, softened (about 1 cup)

Instructions

1. **Mix the Dough**: In a large bowl, combine the flour, sugar, salt, and yeast. Add the eggs and mix until a sticky dough forms. Knead

the dough until it becomes smooth and elastic, about 10 minutes by hand or 5 minutes in a stand mixer.

2. **Incorporate the Butter**: Gradually add the softened butter to the dough, a few pieces at a time, kneading until fully incorporated. The dough will be soft and glossy. Continue kneading for another 5 to 7 minutes until the dough is very smooth.

3. **First Rise**: Place the dough in a greased bowl, cover, and let it rise at room temperature for 1 to 2 hours, or until doubled in size. You can also refrigerate the dough overnight for a slower fermentation.

4. **Shape the Brioche**: After the first rise, turn the dough out onto a floured surface and shape it into a loaf or divide it into smaller pieces to form individual rolls. Place the shaped dough in a

greased loaf pan or on a baking sheet lined with parchment paper.

5. **Second Rise**: Cover the dough and let it rise for another 1 to 2 hours, or until it has puffed up.

6. **Bake**: Preheat the oven to 350°F (175°C). Brush the top of the dough with an egg wash and bake for 25 to 30 minutes for rolls, or 35 to 40 minutes for a loaf, until the top is golden brown.

Challah

Challah is another enriched dough that's traditionally braided. It's slightly less rich than brioche but has a tender crumb and a beautiful golden crust, often made with a touch of honey for sweetness.

7.4 Incorporating Add-ins: Nuts, Seeds, Fruits, and Herbs

Adding flavor and texture to your bread can elevate a simple loaf into something extraordinary. Whether you're folding in nuts and dried fruits for a hearty loaf or incorporating fresh herbs and cheese for a savory twist, learning how to properly incorporate add-ins will expand your bread-making repertoire.

When to Add Ingredients

Add-ins like nuts, seeds, herbs, and fruits should be folded into the dough after the initial mix or during the stretch-and-fold phase. If added too early, they can interfere with gluten development, but if added too late, they may not be evenly distributed throughout the dough.

Common Add-ins and How to Use Them

- **Nuts**: Toasted walnuts, pecans, and almonds add crunch and flavor. Be sure to chop larger nuts to avoid tearing the dough.

- **Seeds**: Sunflower seeds, sesame seeds, flaxseeds, and chia seeds provide a nutritional boost and texture. You can mix seeds directly into the dough or sprinkle them on top before baking.
- **Dried Fruits**: Raisins, dried cranberries, apricots, or figs can add sweetness and chewiness to breads like cinnamon-raisin or holiday fruit loaves.
- **Fresh Herbs**: Rosemary, thyme, and basil are excellent for savory breads. Chop them finely and fold them into the dough.
- **Cheese**: Cheddar, Parmesan, or mozzarella can be incorporated into the dough for cheesy bread or added as a filling for stuffed breads like focaccia or garlic knots.

7.5 Aging, Brining, and Flavor Development

Advanced bread bakers often use techniques like aging dough or brining to develop deeper flavors. These methods slow down the fermentation process, allowing the yeast and bacteria to produce more complex flavors.

Aging Dough
Refrigerating dough overnight, or even for several days, allows for slow fermentation, which enhances both the flavor and texture of the bread. The extended fermentation time gives the yeast more time to work, producing more pronounced flavors, especially in sourdough and other naturally leavened breads.

Brining Dough
Brining, or soaking dough in a saltwater solution, can help enhance flavor, preserve moisture, and improve the dough's texture. This technique is particularly useful for bagels and pretzels, which are boiled in a brine solution before baking to

achieve a chewy texture and shiny crust.

Conclusion: Elevating Your Bread Baking Skills

Advanced bread-making techniques open up a world of possibilities, allowing you to create more complex, flavorful, and visually stunning loaves. Whether you're mastering high-hydration doughs, experimenting with lamination, or incorporating exciting add-ins, these skills will enable you to bake bread that rivals professional bakeries.

Chapter 8:

Troubleshooting Common Bread Issues

Bread making, while rewarding, can sometimes feel frustrating, especially when things don't go as planned. From loaves that don't rise properly to doughs that are too sticky to handle, bread can throw its share of challenges at you. But rest assured— every bread-making issue has a solution.

In this chapter, we'll explore some of the most common problems home bakers encounter and provide troubleshooting tips to help you resolve them. Whether your bread isn't rising, your crust isn't as crispy as you'd like, or your dough is too dense, we've got practical advice to help you get back on track. By the end of this chapter, you'll be equipped to overcome these issues with confidence, turning potential baking disasters into successful loaves.

8.1 Dense or Heavy Bread

One of the most common complaints from home bakers is that their bread comes out too dense or heavy, lacking the light and airy texture they're aiming for. While there are several possible causes, most stem from issues with yeast, gluten development, or proofing.

Common Causes of Dense Bread

- Underproofing: If your dough hasn't had enough time to rise properly, the yeast won't produce enough gas to create the light texture you want. Underproofed dough results in bread that's too dense because the gluten hasn't stretched out enough to trap the gas.
- Too Much Flour: Adding too much flour during mixing or kneading can lead to dense bread. While it's tempting to add more flour if the dough feels sticky, this can result in a dry dough that's

difficult to rise and produces a dense crumb.

- Poor Gluten Development: Kneading helps develop the gluten network that gives bread its structure. If your dough isn't kneaded enough, the gluten won't be strong enough to trap the gas produced by the yeast, leading to a denser loaf.

How to Fix Dense Bread

- Extend Proofing Time: Be patient with your dough and let it rise until it has doubled in size. A longer rise time at a cooler temperature can also help develop flavor and texture. Check your dough by pressing your finger into it—if the indentation springs back slowly, it's ready to bake.
- Use Proper Flour Measurements: Avoid packing flour into measuring cups, which can result in using too much. Instead,

spoon the flour into the cup and level it off. Better yet, use a kitchen scale for accurate measurements.

- Improve Kneading Technique: Make sure you're kneading the dough long enough to develop the gluten. If you're not sure, perform the "windowpane test" by stretching a small piece of dough—if it forms a thin, translucent membrane without tearing, the gluten is well developed.

8.2 Bread that Doesn't Rise Properly

Another common issue is bread that doesn't rise enough during proofing or baking, resulting in a flat, dense loaf. This problem can stem from inactive yeast, incorrect proofing times, or even environmental factors.

Common Causes of Poor Rise

- Inactive Yeast: Yeast can lose its potency if it's old or stored improperly. If your yeast is no longer active, it won't create the gas needed for the dough to rise.
- Cold or Hot Water: Yeast thrives in warm temperatures. If the water or liquid you're using is too cold, it can slow down yeast activity. On the other hand, water that's too hot can kill the yeast.
- Underproofing or Overproofing: If the dough hasn't been given enough time to rise, or if it has been left too long, the rise can be insufficient. Underproofed dough will be tight and dense, while overproofed dough can collapse when baked.

How to Fix Poor Rise

- Check Your Yeast: Make sure your yeast is fresh and active. If using active dry yeast, dissolve it in warm water (about 110°F/45°C) and check for bubbles after 5 to 10 minutes. If it doesn't foam up, your yeast may be inactive, and you'll need to start with fresh yeast.
- Use the Right Water Temperature: When mixing yeast with water, aim for a temperature between 100°F and 110°F (38°C to 43°C). Too cold, and the yeast will be sluggish; too hot, and the yeast will die.
- Proper Proofing: Keep an eye on your dough while it's rising. A properly proofed dough should double in size. To test, press your finger into the dough—if the indentation springs back slowly, it's ready. If it springs back quickly, let it rise longer. If it doesn't spring back at all, it may be overproofed.

8.3 Dough That's Too Sticky or Too Dry

Dough that's too sticky can be difficult to handle and shape, while dough that's too dry can result in bread that doesn't rise well and has a dense texture. Getting the right dough consistency is key to successful bread making.

Common Causes of Sticky Dough

- Too Much Water: Adding too much water can create a sticky dough that's difficult to knead and shape.
- High Humidity: Humidity in your kitchen can affect the dough's hydration. On humid days, flour absorbs moisture from the air, making the dough stickier.

Common Causes of Dry Dough

- Too Much Flour: Over-flouring the dough can lead to dryness. If the dough feels too sticky, it's tempting to keep adding flour, but this can result in a stiff dough that's difficult to rise and shape.

How to Fix Sticky Dough

- Flour Your Work Surface Lightly: Use just enough flour on your work surface to prevent sticking, but avoid over-flouring. The dough will become less sticky as you knead it and the gluten develops.
- Use the Stretch and Fold Technique: Instead of adding more flour, try using the stretch-and-fold method to strengthen the dough. This technique helps build structure without requiring additional flour.

How to Fix Dry Dough

- Add Water Gradually: If your dough feels dry, add water 1 tablespoon at a time while kneading, until it reaches the right consistency. Be cautious not to overdo it, as too much water can make the dough too sticky.

8.4 Flat or Deflated Loaves

Flat or deflated loaves can happen for several reasons, ranging from incorrect proofing to improper shaping. Often, the problem lies in how the dough was handled during its final rise or how it was baked.

Common Causes of Flat Loaves

- Overproofing: When dough is left to rise for too long, the gluten structure weakens, and the dough can collapse, resulting in a flat loaf.
- Improper Shaping: If the dough isn't shaped correctly, it won't have the tension needed to hold its shape during baking.

- No Steam During Baking: For breads like baguettes or rustic loaves, steam in the oven helps create a crisp crust and allows the dough to expand fully. Without steam, the loaf can spread out instead of rising upward.

How to Fix Flat Loaves

- Avoid Overproofing: Keep an eye on your dough during the final rise. If it starts to overproof, you may notice the dough feels overly soft or starts to deflate. Aim to bake the dough when it has doubled in size but still feels resilient to the touch.
- Shape the Dough Properly: When shaping your dough, create surface tension by folding the dough tightly and tucking the edges under. This gives the dough structure and helps it rise upward instead of outward.

- Create Steam in the Oven: To encourage oven spring and get a good rise, bake bread with steam. You can place a pan of water in the oven or spray the inside of the oven with water just before baking.

8.5 Crust That's Too Hard or Too Soft

Getting the perfect crust on your bread can be tricky. Sometimes the crust is too hard and thick, while other times it's too soft and pale. The crust is influenced by factors like baking time, temperature, and moisture levels.

Common Causes of Hard Crust

- **Overbaking**: Baking bread for too long or at too high a temperature can result in a thick, hard crust. This is particularly common in lean breads that don't contain fats like butter or oil, which naturally soften the crust.

- **Too Much Flour**: Dusting too much flour on the surface of the dough before baking can lead to a dry, hard crust. While some flour is needed to prevent sticking, an excess can create a dry exterior that hardens during baking.

Common Causes of Soft Crust

- **Underbaking**: If bread isn't baked for long enough or at a high enough temperature, the crust won't have time to fully crisp up. This can leave the loaf with a soft, pale exterior, even if the inside is fully baked.
- **Lack of Steam**: Steam plays a crucial role in creating a crispy crust, particularly for breads like baguettes, sourdough, and ciabatta. Without steam, the crust may not develop properly, resulting in a soft, chewy outer layer rather than a crisp one.

How to Fix a Hard Crust

- **Lower the Baking Temperature**: If you find your bread is developing too hard of a crust, consider lowering the oven temperature by 10-15°F and increasing the baking time slightly. This will give the bread time to cook through without toughening the crust.
- **Brush the Crust with Butter or Oil**: After baking, brushing the crust with melted butter, olive oil, or even milk can soften a hard exterior. This is especially helpful for enriched breads like brioche or challah.

How to Fix a Soft Crust

- **Increase Baking Time**: If your bread has a soft, pale crust, extend the baking time by 5 to 10 minutes. To avoid overbaking the inside, you can tent the loaf with aluminum foil toward the end of the bake to prevent excess browning while allowing the crust to crisp up.
- **Bake with Steam**: If your bread needs a crisp crust, create steam in your oven by placing a pan of water

on the bottom rack while the bread bakes, or by spraying water inside the oven during the first few minutes of baking. This will allow the crust to set before the moisture evaporates.

8.6 Bread Tearing or Collapsing During Baking

It can be disappointing to see your beautifully risen dough collapse in the oven. Bread that tears, bursts, or collapses while baking can be a result of underproofing, improper scoring, or weak dough structure.

Common Causes of Collapsed Bread

- **Overproofing**: If the dough is allowed to rise too much before baking, it can exhaust the yeast and lose its ability to hold its shape. Overproofed dough often collapses during baking, resulting in a dense, deflated loaf.

- **Underproofing**: On the flip side, underproofed dough hasn't had enough time to develop sufficient gas and gluten structure. As a result, the dough doesn't have enough strength to rise properly in the oven and may tear or collapse.
- **Improper Scoring**: Scoring (cutting shallow slashes into the dough) allows bread to expand evenly during baking. If you skip this step or score too lightly, the dough can burst unevenly, creating unsightly tears or misshapen loaves.

How to Fix Collapsed Bread

- **Monitor Proofing More Closely**: Check your dough frequently during the final rise. Properly proofed dough should spring back slowly when you press your finger into it, but if it deflates immediately or feels too soft, it may be overproofed. Conversely, if it doesn't spring back at all, it needs more time.

- **Score Correctly**: Use a sharp knife or bread lame to make decisive cuts in the dough before baking. This allows the bread to expand where you want it to, avoiding bursts and tears. Make sure your scores are about ¼ inch deep for most breads.

8.7 Uneven Texture or Crumb

The texture or "crumb" of your bread refers to the arrangement of air pockets within the loaf. Ideally, you want your bread to have a consistent crumb, with even air distribution. If your bread has large, uneven holes, or if the inside is too dense or gummy, there are a few common culprits.

Common Causes of Uneven Texture

- **Inconsistent Kneading**: Proper kneading is essential for developing gluten, which creates the structure needed for an even crumb. Inconsistent kneading can lead to areas of the dough with weak

gluten, resulting in uneven air pockets.
- **Underproofing**: If dough is not given enough time to rise properly, the gluten network won't be strong enough to hold the gas produced by the yeast, leading to an uneven crumb.
- **Shaping Issues**: Poor shaping can also result in uneven crumbs. If the dough isn't shaped properly, large air pockets can become trapped, leading to irregular holes in the final loaf.

How to Fix Uneven Texture

- **Knead Thoroughly**: Ensure that you knead the dough long enough to develop a strong gluten network. If using a stand mixer, knead for about 8 to 10 minutes; if kneading by hand, aim for 10 to 15 minutes. A well-kneaded dough should pass the "windowpane test," where you can stretch a small piece of dough into a thin, translucent sheet without tearing it.

- **Allow for Proper Proofing**: Let the dough rise fully during both the bulk fermentation and final proofing stages. This ensures that the yeast has enough time to create the gas needed for an even crumb.
- **Shape the Dough Correctly**: When shaping your loaf, gently press out any large air bubbles before forming the final shape. Proper tension in the dough will help create an even crumb and prevent large, irregular air pockets.

8.8 Bread That's Gummy or Undercooked

Biting into bread that looks golden on the outside but is gummy or doughy on the inside can be a frustrating experience. Undercooked bread can occur if the baking time is too short, the oven temperature is incorrect, or if the dough itself was mishandled.

Common Causes of Gummy Bread

- **Baking Temperature Too Low**: If your oven isn't hot enough, the bread's interior may not cook through fully before the crust sets, leaving the inside gummy or raw.
- **Underbaking**: Even if the crust looks done, the inside may need more time to bake. This is especially true for larger loaves or high-hydration doughs, which need extra time in the oven.
- **Overmixing or Overproofing**: Overmixing or allowing dough to overproof can break down the gluten structure, preventing the bread from setting properly during baking.

How to Fix Gummy Bread

- **Bake at the Correct Temperature**: Make sure your oven is properly preheated to the temperature indicated in the recipe. For most breads, this is between 375°F and 450°F (190°C and 230°C). Use an oven thermometer if necessary to verify the oven's accuracy.

- **Extend the Baking Time**: If you notice that your bread's crust is browning too quickly but the inside isn't fully cooked, cover the loaf with aluminum foil and continue baking for another 10 to 15 minutes. This will allow the interior to bake through without burning the crust.
- **Test for Doneness**: Use a kitchen thermometer to check if your bread is fully baked. Insert the thermometer into the center of the loaf; for most breads, the internal temperature should be between 190°F and 210°F (88°C and 99°C) when fully baked.

Conclusion: The Path to Perfect Bread

Bread making is a learning process, and even experienced bakers encounter issues from time to time. The key to overcoming common bread problems is to understand what went wrong and how to fix it. By adjusting proofing times, improving your kneading techniques, and paying attention to baking temperatures, you can prevent many of these issues and turn out consistently delicious loaves.

Troubleshooting may seem daunting at first, but with practice, you'll develop an intuition for your dough and an understanding of how to adjust your techniques based on the results. Each loaf you bake, even the imperfect ones, will teach you something new.

In the next chapter, we'll delve into storage and serving tips, so you can keep your homemade bread fresh and make the most of every slice.

Chapter 9:

Creative Additions and Variations

Bread, in its simplest form, consists of just four ingredients: flour, water, yeast, and salt. However, once you've mastered the basics, bread becomes a blank canvas for creativity. Whether you want to add flavors, textures, or nutritional value, there are endless possibilities for customizing your homemade loaves with ingredients like herbs, nuts, seeds, spices, fruits, and even vegetables.

In this chapter, we'll explore how to incorporate various additions into your bread to create unique flavors and textures. You'll learn the best techniques for mixing in ingredients without compromising the structure of your dough, and we'll provide you with some exciting recipes to inspire your bread-making adventures. By the end of this chapter, you'll be ready to experiment and develop your own signature bread recipes.

9.1 Adding Flavor with Herbs and Spices

Herbs and spices are one of the easiest ways to enhance the flavor of your bread. Whether you're baking a savory loaf to accompany a meal or a spiced bread for a special occasion, the right combination of seasonings can transform a simple bread into something truly extraordinary.

Choosing the Right Herbs and Spices

The choice of herbs and spices depends on the type of bread you're making and the flavors you want to highlight. Fresh herbs like rosemary, thyme, parsley, and basil are excellent in savory breads, while dried spices like cinnamon, nutmeg, cardamom, and cloves are often used in sweet breads. Garlic, onion, cumin, and chili powder can add bold, savory notes, while citrus zest, vanilla, and ginger bring brightness and warmth to sweeter breads.

How to Incorporate Herbs and Spices into Dough

- **Fresh Herbs**: Chop fresh herbs finely before adding them to the dough to ensure even distribution. For most breads, about 1 to 2 tablespoons of fresh herbs is sufficient.

- **Dried Herbs and Spices**: Dried herbs are more concentrated than fresh, so you'll need less— about 1 to 2 teaspoons per loaf. Dried spices can be mixed into the dough along with the dry ingredients, but be mindful of their strength; a little goes a long way.
- **Infusing Oils**: For a more subtle herb flavor, try infusing your oil with herbs before adding it to the dough. Heat olive oil with rosemary, thyme, or garlic, and allow it to cool before mixing it into the dough for a delicate, aromatic flavor.

9.2 Nuts and Seeds for Texture and Nutrition

Nuts and seeds not only add a satisfying crunch to your bread but also provide extra nutrients like healthy fats, protein, and fiber. Whether you're folding walnuts into a hearty whole wheat loaf or sprinkling sunflower seeds on top of a rustic sourdough, these ingredients bring texture and depth to your bread.

Common Nuts and Seeds to Use

- **Nuts**: Walnuts, pecans, almonds, and hazelnuts are popular choices for bread. They add richness and a subtle sweetness. Toasting nuts before adding them to the dough enhances their flavor.
- **Seeds**: Sunflower seeds, sesame seeds, poppy seeds, flaxseeds, chia seeds, and pumpkin seeds are commonly used in bread. Seeds can be mixed into the dough or sprinkled on top for added crunch.

How to Incorporate Nuts and Seeds

- **Folding In**: To prevent nuts and seeds from disrupting the gluten structure, fold them into the dough after the initial kneading or during the stretch-and-fold process. Aim for about ½ to 1 cup of nuts or seeds per loaf, depending on your preference.
- **Topping**: Seeds make a beautiful and nutritious topping for bread. After shaping the dough, brush the top with water, milk, or egg wash, and sprinkle generously with seeds. Press them lightly into the surface to help them adhere during baking.

9.3 Using Dried Fruits and Sweet Additions

Dried fruits like raisins, cranberries, apricots, and figs add sweetness and chewiness to bread. They are especially popular in enriched doughs, holiday breads, and breakfast loaves. The natural sugars in dried fruits caramelize during baking, creating pockets of sweetness that complement the bread's flavor.

Common Dried Fruits to Use

- **Raisins**: A classic choice for sweet breads, especially in cinnamon raisin bread or holiday panettone.
- **Cranberries**: Their tartness balances the sweetness in breads like cranberry walnut or cranberry orange loaves.
- **Apricots and Figs**: These fruits add rich, earthy sweetness to breads, especially when paired with nuts or whole grains.
- **Dates and Prunes**: Naturally sweet and sticky, dates and prunes work well in rich, hearty breads and can even be pureed to replace some of the sugar in a recipe.

How to Incorporate Dried Fruits

- **Soaking**: Soaking dried fruits in warm water or juice for 10 to 15 minutes before adding them to the dough softens them and prevents them from drawing moisture from the dough. You can also soak fruits in alcohol (like rum or brandy) for a more intense flavor.
- **Folding In**: Like nuts and seeds, dried fruits should be folded into the dough after kneading. If you're adding multiple types of fruit, aim for a total of about 1 cup per loaf.

9.4 Incorporating Cheese for Savory Breads

Cheese is a fantastic addition to savory breads, adding richness, saltiness, and a gooey or crispy texture depending on the type of cheese used. From cheddar in rustic loaves to Parmesan in focaccia, cheese can take your bread to the next level.

Best Cheeses for Bread

- **Cheddar**: Sharp cheddar pairs beautifully with herbs, garlic, and onions. It melts well, creating pockets of cheesy goodness throughout the bread.
- **Parmesan**: Hard cheeses like Parmesan add a savory, nutty flavor and a crisp, golden crust when sprinkled on top of the dough before baking.
- **Feta**: This crumbly cheese works well in Mediterranean-style breads, especially when combined with olives, sun-dried tomatoes, or herbs like oregano and thyme.
- **Mozzarella**: For stuffed breads or pizza-style loaves, mozzarella provides a stretchy, melty texture.

How to Incorporate Cheese

- **Folding and Layering**: Fold small cubes or shreds of cheese into the dough after the first kneading. You can also layer cheese in between folds during shaping for a swirled effect.
- **Topping**: Sprinkle grated cheese over the surface of the dough just before baking for a crispy, cheesy topping. This works particularly well with hard cheeses like Parmesan or Pecorino.

9.5 Vegetables and Whole Grains for Hearty, Wholesome Breads

For those looking to create more wholesome, nutrient-dense breads, adding vegetables and whole grains is an excellent option. Vegetables like carrots, zucchini, and sweet potatoes contribute moisture, sweetness, and nutrition, while whole grains like oats, barley, and quinoa add fiber, texture, and depth of flavor.

Incorporating Vegetables

- **Grated Vegetables**: Vegetables like carrots, zucchini, and beets can be grated and folded into the dough. They add moisture and a subtle sweetness while keeping the bread soft and tender.
- **Mashed Vegetables**: Mashed sweet potatoes, pumpkin, or butternut squash can be mixed directly into the dough. These vegetables lend a smooth texture and a slight sweetness, perfect for hearty, rustic breads.
- **Roasted Vegetables**: For more intense flavor, try folding roasted vegetables (like caramelized onions, roasted garlic, or peppers) into the dough.

Whole Grains

- **Oats**: Oats add heartiness and chew to breads. Use rolled oats for a softer texture or steel-cut oats for a more substantial bite. Oats can be mixed into the dough or sprinkled on top.
- **Barley and Quinoa**: Cooked barley or quinoa can be added to the dough for a chewy texture and extra fiber. Be sure to cool the grains before incorporating them to avoid interfering with the dough's fermentation.
- **Flaxseed and Chia Seeds**: These tiny seeds are packed with nutrients and can be mixed into the dough or used as a topping. Chia seeds, when hydrated, also help keep bread moist.

9.6 Sweet Breads and Dessert Loaves

Sweet breads and dessert loaves blur the line between bread and cake, offering a rich, indulgent treat. These breads are often enriched with butter, eggs, sugar, and spices, and can be flavored with everything from chocolate chips to cinnamon and nuts.

Popular Sweet Bread Varieties

- **Cinnamon Rolls**: A classic sweet bread, cinnamon rolls are made from an enriched dough filled with cinnamon sugar, rolled up, and baked until golden brown. They're often topped with cream cheese or vanilla icing.
- **Chocolate Babka**: This Eastern European bread features layers of rich, chocolatey filling swirled through a soft, buttery dough. It's perfect for special occasions or a decadent dessert.
- **Lemon Poppy Seed Bread**: Bright and zesty, lemon poppy seed bread combines the tartness of lemon with the crunch of poppy seeds, often finished with a sweet lemon glaze.

- **Fruit-Filled Braids**: Braided loaves filled with fruit preserves or jams, like raspberry or apricot, are both visually stunning and delicious.

How to Create Sweet Breads

- **Enriching the Dough**: Sweet breads often require an enriched dough, made with butter, eggs, and sugar. These ingredients create a tender crumb and a rich flavor.
- **Adding Fillings**: For breads like cinnamon rolls or babka, the filling is spread over the rolled-out dough, which is then rolled up and sliced before baking. Be generous with fillings like cinnamon sugar, chocolate, or fruit preserves to ensure every bite is flavorful.

Conclusion: Expanding Your Bread Making Repertoire

Once you've mastered the basics of bread making, the possibilities for customization are endless. Whether you're adding herbs, spices, nuts, or fruits, or experimenting with vegetables, cheese, and whole grains, each loaf can be a unique creation. These creative additions not only enhance the flavor and texture of your bread but also offer a way to make your loaves more nutritious and exciting.

In the next chapter, we'll tackle some of the common issues bakers face and offer troubleshooting tips to ensure that your bread-making journey continues smoothly.

Chapter 10:

Storing and Serving Bread

There's nothing quite like the satisfaction of pulling a perfectly baked loaf of bread from the oven, letting it cool just enough, and slicing into it to reveal a soft, airy crumb and a golden crust. But once your bread is baked, what happens next? Storing and serving your bread properly is essential to maintaining its freshness, texture, and flavor. Whether you're enjoying your bread fresh from the oven or preserving it for later, knowing the right techniques will help you get the most out of every loaf you bake.

In this chapter, we'll explore the best ways to store your homemade bread, tips for freezing it, and methods for reheating it while keeping it delicious. We'll also cover creative serving suggestions and ways to use up leftover bread, so nothing goes to waste.

10.1 Storing Fresh Bread

Freshly baked bread is best enjoyed the day it's made, especially when it's still warm with a crisp crust. However, homemade bread doesn't have the preservatives that store-bought bread does, so it can dry out or become stale quickly if not stored properly.

Room Temperature Storage
For most types of bread, room temperature storage is ideal if you plan to eat the bread within a few days. Keeping bread at room temperature helps preserve the texture and flavor without the risk of condensation forming inside the packaging, which can make the bread soggy.

How to Store Bread at Room Temperature

1. **For Crusty Breads** (like sourdough, baguettes, or

ciabatta): Crusty bread should be
stored uncovered or in a paper
bag for the first day to maintain
its crisp exterior. After that,
loosely wrap the bread in a clean
kitchen towel or store it in a
paper bag to keep it from drying
out completely. Avoid airtight
containers, as they can trap
moisture and cause the crust to
become soft.

2. **For Soft Breads** (like sandwich
loaves, challah, or brioche): Soft
breads benefit from being stored
in airtight containers or plastic
bags to keep the crumb tender
and prevent drying. For best
results, store the loaf whole and
slice it as needed to retain
moisture in the loaf.

Storing Bread in a Bread Box

A bread box is a great tool for keeping
bread fresh at room temperature. It
provides a balance between airflow
and moisture retention, allowing the

bread to breathe without drying out too quickly. A good bread box will help keep the crust of your bread firm while maintaining a moist, tender crumb inside.

How Long Can Bread Be Stored at Room Temperature?

- **Crusty Breads**: Best within 1 to 2 days but can last up to 3 days with proper storage.
- **Soft Breads**: Can stay fresh for up to 4 to 5 days if stored in an airtight container.

10.2 Freezing Bread for Long-Term Storage

If you've baked more bread than you can eat in a few days, freezing is the best way to preserve it for future use. Bread freezes exceptionally well, and with the right method, you can enjoy it for weeks without losing quality. Freezing your bread also allows you to bake in bulk and save time.

How to Freeze Whole Loaves

1. **Cool the Bread Completely**:
   Before freezing, make sure your
   bread has cooled completely.
   Freezing warm bread can cause
   condensation to form inside the
   packaging, leading to freezer
   burn and a soggy texture when
   thawed.
2. **Wrap the Loaf**: Wrap the bread
   tightly in plastic wrap or
   aluminum foil. For added
   protection, place the wrapped
   loaf in a resealable plastic freezer
   bag. Removing as much air as
   possible from the bag will help
   prevent freezer burn.
3. **Label and Date**: It's easy to
   forget when you froze your
   bread, so label the package with
   the date. Most bread can be
   frozen for up to 3 months without
   a significant loss in quality.

How to Freeze Sliced Bread
Freezing sliced bread is a convenient

option if you want to be able to grab individual slices for toast or sandwiches without thawing the entire loaf.

1. **Slice the Bread**: Once the bread has cooled, slice it into even slices.
2. **Flash Freeze**: Lay the slices out on a baking sheet in a single layer and place them in the freezer for 1 to 2 hours. Once the slices are frozen, transfer them to a resealable plastic freezer bag. This prevents the slices from sticking together, so you can remove them one at a time.
3. **Label and Date**: As with whole loaves, label the bag with the date. Frozen sliced bread can also last up to 3 months in the freezer.

10.3 Reheating and Refreshing Bread

Frozen or day-old bread can easily be refreshed to bring back its freshly baked quality. Whether you're reheating a whole loaf or just a slice, there are simple methods to restore bread to its original softness and crispness.

Reheating Whole Loaves
To reheat a whole frozen or day-old loaf, follow these steps:

1. **Thaw the Bread**: If the bread is frozen, let it thaw at room temperature for a few hours or overnight.
2. **Wrap in Foil**: Preheat your oven to 350°F (175°C). Wrap the thawed loaf in aluminum foil to prevent it from drying out.
3. **Bake for 10 to 15 Minutes**: Place the wrapped loaf in the oven and bake for 10 to 15 minutes. This will warm the bread through and revive its texture.

4. **Unwrap for the Last 5 Minutes**: For a crusty loaf, remove the foil for the last 5 minutes of baking to allow the crust to crisp up again.

Reheating Sliced Bread
For frozen or day-old slices of bread:

1. **Toast or Oven Method**: Pop individual slices into the toaster or place them in a preheated 350°F (175°C) oven for 5 to 7 minutes until they're warmed through and lightly toasted.
2. **Microwave Method**: You can also microwave a slice of bread wrapped in a damp paper towel for 10 to 15 seconds to soften it, though this method may not restore crispness.

10.4 Creative Serving Ideas for Fresh and Leftover Bread

Bread is incredibly versatile, and there are endless ways to enjoy it beyond simply serving slices at the dinner table. Here are some creative ideas for serving fresh and leftover bread, ensuring that none of it goes to waste.

Fresh Bread

- **Bread Boards**: Create an impressive bread board with a variety of homemade loaves, sliced and served with an array of spreads like butter, olive oil, flavored dips, and cheeses. Freshly baked bread pairs perfectly with charcuterie, roasted vegetables, or pâté.
- **Toast Toppings**: Take your morning toast to the next level with creative toppings. Avocado toast, ricotta with honey, smoked salmon with cream cheese, or nut butter with sliced fruit are all delicious options.
- **Bread Bowls**: For a fun presentation, hollow out round

loaves of bread to create bowls for soups, chili, or dips. This works especially well with dense, sturdy breads like sourdough.

Leftover Bread
If you have leftover bread that's starting to go stale, don't throw it away! There are countless ways to use up day-old bread.

- **Croutons**: Turn stale bread into homemade croutons by cutting it into cubes, tossing with olive oil and herbs, and baking at 375°F (190°C) for 10 to 15 minutes until crispy. They're perfect for adding crunch to soups or salads.
- **Bread Pudding**: Day-old bread is the ideal base for bread pudding, a comforting dessert made by soaking the bread in a mixture of eggs, milk, sugar, and spices, then baking until golden and custardy. You can make sweet versions with cinnamon,

raisins, and vanilla, or savory versions with cheese and herbs.

- **French Toast**: Stale bread makes the best French toast because it soaks up the egg mixture without becoming too soggy. Dip slices in a mix of eggs, milk, sugar, and vanilla, then fry until golden brown. Top with syrup, fresh fruit, or powdered sugar.
- **Panade**: Panade is a savory French dish that uses layers of stale bread, broth, and vegetables or meat, baked into a flavorful casserole. It's a great way to repurpose bread into a hearty meal.
- **Breadcrumbs**: Pulse stale bread in a food processor to make homemade breadcrumbs. Use them to coat chicken or fish, sprinkle on top of casseroles, or mix into meatballs or stuffing.

10.5 Extending the Shelf Life: Avoiding Mold and Staleness

Mold and staleness are two common problems that occur when storing bread. While staleness is inevitable over time, you can extend the life of your bread by storing it properly. Mold, on the other hand, is a sign of too much moisture and should be avoided entirely.

Preventing Mold

- **Keep Bread Dry**: Moisture encourages mold growth, so it's essential to store bread in a dry environment. Avoid sealing warm bread in plastic, as it will trap moisture inside.
- **Use Paper Bags or Bread Boxes**: As mentioned earlier, paper bags and bread boxes allow the bread to breathe, preventing mold while keeping the crust crisp.

- **Freeze If Necessary**: If you don't plan to eat the bread within a few days, freezing is the best option to prevent mold.

Dealing with Staleness

- **Refresh in the Oven**: If your bread has gone stale but hasn't developed mold, you can refresh it by reheating it in the oven as described earlier in the chapter. This will restore the bread's softness and give the crust new life.

Conclusion: Making the Most of Every Loaf

Storing and serving your bread properly ensures that you get the most out of every loaf you bake. By learning the best techniques for storing bread at room temperature, freezing it for later, and refreshing it for serving, you can enjoy your homemade bread at its peak flavor and texture.

And when it comes to using up leftover bread, the possibilities are endless. Whether you're making croutons, French toast, or a comforting bread pudding, there's no reason for any of your bread to go to waste. With these tips in mind, you'll be able to make, store, and enjoy your homemade bread to its fullest.

In the next chapter, we'll explore specialty bread recipes and techniques from around the world, allowing you to expand your baking repertoire and continue your bread-making journey.

Chapter 11:

Specialty Breads from Around the World

Bread, in its many forms, has been a cornerstone of diets across the globe for thousands of years. Each culture has its own unique variations, shaped by local ingredients, customs, and traditions. Exploring the diverse world of bread can expand your baking horizons and introduce you to new flavors and techniques. From airy flatbreads to hearty loaves, the world's specialty breads offer an exciting opportunity to add global flair to your kitchen.

In this chapter, we'll take a journey through several regions, highlighting some of the most beloved breads from around the world. You'll find easy-to-follow recipes and tips on how to master each one, along with a glimpse into the cultural significance of these iconic breads.

11.1 French Baguette: The Quintessential Artisan Loaf

No discussion of international bread would be complete without mentioning the classic French baguette. Long, thin, and golden-crusted, the baguette is synonymous with French culture and cuisine. Known for its crisp exterior and light, airy crumb, the baguette requires simple ingredients but careful technique.

Ingredients

- 500g bread flour (about 4 cups)
- 325g water (about 1 ⅓ cups)
- 10g salt (about 1 ½ tsp)
- 5g instant yeast (about 1 ½ tsp)

Instructions

1. **Mix the Dough**: In a large bowl, combine the flour, salt, and yeast. Slowly add the water, mixing until the dough comes together. Let it rest for 15 minutes to allow the flour to hydrate.
2. **Knead and Bulk Ferment**: Knead the dough for 8-10 minutes, then place it in a greased bowl to rise for 1-2

hours, or until it has doubled in size.

3. **Shape and Final Rise**: Divide the dough into three equal parts and shape each one into a long, slender loaf. Place the shaped dough onto a baking sheet lined with parchment paper, cover, and let it rise for 45 minutes.

4. **Score and Bake**: Preheat the oven to 475°F (245°C). Score each loaf with a few diagonal slashes and bake for 20-25 minutes, or until the crust is golden brown.

Cultural Significance

The baguette is a symbol of French culture and daily life. Often bought fresh from bakeries, it's common to see Parisians carrying them home tucked under their arm. In France, baguettes are so cherished that they are protected by law—the "Décret Pain" regulates how they must be made to bear the name "baguette."

11.2 Indian Naan: The Pillowy Flatbread

Naan is a soft, slightly chewy flatbread that is a staple in Indian cuisine. Traditionally cooked in a tandoor oven, naan is perfect for scooping up curries and stews or serving alongside grilled meats. The dough is enriched with yogurt and sometimes milk, which gives naan its signature soft texture.

Ingredients

- 400g all-purpose flour (about 3 ¼ cups)
- 100g plain yogurt (about ½ cup)
- 150g warm water (about ⅔ cup)
- 1 tsp salt
- 2 tsp instant yeast
- 1 tbsp olive oil
- 1 tbsp melted butter (for brushing)

Instructions

1. **Mix the Dough**: In a large mixing bowl, combine the flour, salt, and yeast. Add the yogurt, warm water, and olive oil, stirring until a dough forms.
2. **Knead and Rise**: Knead the dough for 5-7 minutes until smooth, then let it rise in a greased bowl for about an hour, or until it doubles in size.
3. **Shape the Naan**: After the dough has risen, divide it into 8 equal portions. Roll each piece into an oval shape about ¼ inch thick.
4. **Cook the Naan**: Preheat a skillet over high heat. Cook each naan for 1-2 minutes on one side, until bubbles form, then flip and cook the other side for another minute. Brush with melted butter before serving.

Cultural Significance
Naan is traditionally cooked in a tandoor, a cylindrical clay oven, which

gives it a unique, slightly charred flavor. Naan is an essential part of Indian meals, often served with rich dishes like chicken tikka masala or butter chicken. It's also versatile enough to be stuffed with fillings like cheese or minced meat for added variety.

11.3 Middle Eastern Pita: The Perfect Pocket Bread

Pita bread is a versatile Middle Eastern flatbread that puffs up during baking to form a pocket, making it ideal for stuffing with fillings like falafel, hummus, or grilled vegetables. Its simple ingredients and quick baking time make it an easy, go-to bread for home bakers.

Ingredients

- 450g all-purpose flour (about 3 ½ cups)
- 300g water (about 1 ¼ cups)

- 2 tsp salt
- 2 tsp instant yeast
- 1 tbsp olive oil

Instructions

1. **Mix the Dough**: In a large bowl, combine the flour, yeast, and salt. Slowly add the water and olive oil, stirring until a dough forms.
2. **Knead and First Rise**: Knead the dough for 8-10 minutes until smooth and elastic, then let it rise for 1 hour, or until doubled in size.
3. **Shape and Bake**: Divide the dough into 8 pieces and roll each into a round, about ¼ inch thick. Preheat your oven to 475°F (245°C) with a baking stone or inverted baking sheet inside. Bake the pitas on the hot stone for 3-4 minutes, until they puff up. Flip and bake for another minute.

Cultural Significance
Pita is one of the most ancient forms of bread, with its origins tracing back thousands of years. It remains a staple across the Middle East, often used to scoop up dips like hummus or baba ghanoush. Its ability to puff up and create a natural pocket makes it ideal for sandwiches, and its soft, pillowy texture complements a variety of fillings.

11.4 Mexican Bolillos: The Versatile Roll

Bolillos are small, oval-shaped rolls that are often referred to as Mexico's answer to the French baguette. Crispy on the outside and soft on the inside, bolillos are a popular choice for making tortas, a type of Mexican sandwich filled with meats, beans, avocado, and more.

Ingredients

- 500g bread flour (about 4 cups)

- 300g warm water (about 1 ¼ cups)
- 10g salt (about 1 ½ tsp)
- 10g instant yeast (about 2 ¼ tsp)
- 1 tbsp sugar

Instructions

1. **Mix the Dough**: Combine the flour, yeast, salt, and sugar in a large bowl. Gradually add the water and mix until a dough forms.
2. **Knead and First Rise**: Knead the dough for 8-10 minutes, then allow it to rise in a greased bowl for 1-2 hours, or until doubled in size.
3. **Shape the Bolillos**: Divide the dough into 8 pieces. Shape each piece into an oval by folding the edges toward the center and rolling it into a football shape. Place the rolls on a parchment-lined baking sheet and let them rise for another hour.

4. **Bake**: Preheat your oven to 450°F (230°C). Score the tops of the bolillos with a sharp knife and bake for 20-25 minutes, or until golden brown.

Cultural Significance

Bolillos are ubiquitous in Mexican bakeries and homes, often enjoyed fresh with butter or used to make sandwiches (tortas). They are particularly famous as the bread for tortas ahogadas, a specialty of Guadalajara in which bolillos are drowned in a spicy tomato sauce. Their crusty exterior and soft crumb make them the perfect bread for soaking up sauces and fillings.

11.5 Ethiopian Injera: A Sourdough Flatbread

Injera is a spongy, sour flatbread made from teff flour that serves as both a plate and utensil in Ethiopian and Eritrean cuisine. Its tangy flavor pairs well with rich stews and vegetable dishes, and its porous texture is perfect for soaking up sauces.

Ingredients

- 2 cups teff flour
- 2 ½ cups water
- 1 tsp salt

Instructions

1. **Prepare the Batter**: In a large bowl, mix the teff flour and water. Cover the bowl with a clean kitchen towel and let it sit at room temperature for 1-3 days to ferment. The batter will develop a sour smell, which is a sign of fermentation.
2. **Cook the Injera**: After fermentation, add the salt and mix the batter. Preheat a nonstick skillet or griddle over medium heat. Pour about ½ cup of batter onto the hot skillet,

swirling it around to cover the surface in a thin layer.

3. **Cook Until Bubbles Form**: Let the injera cook until bubbles form on the surface and the edges begin to lift. There's no need to flip—injera is cooked on one side only. Once it's done, transfer to a plate and let it cool.

Cultural Significance

Injera is an integral part of Ethiopian meals, often used as both a base and a utensil for eating dishes like doro wat (chicken stew) and misir wat (spiced lentils). The communal nature of sharing a large piece of injera with multiple dishes placed on top encourages family-style eating and conversation.

Conclusion: Exploring the World Through Bread

Exploring the breads of the world offers an incredible opportunity to understand the rich cultural history behind this staple food. From the crisp French baguette to the pillowy naan of India, each bread tells a story of the people and traditions that shaped it. By mastering these global breads, you not only expand your baking skills but also bring a taste of different cultures into your home.

In the next chapter, we'll explore more about using specialized techniques and tools to take your bread-making skills to an even higher level, allowing you to create artisanal-quality bread with confidence.

Chapter 12:

Your Bread-Making Journey Continues

As you reach the end of this book, you've explored the vast and fascinating world of bread making. From mastering the basics to exploring global bread traditions and tackling advanced techniques, you've gained a deeper understanding of the art and science behind one of humanity's most essential and beloved foods. But the beautiful thing about bread is that there is always something new to learn, try, and enjoy. This chapter serves as both a conclusion and a celebration of your journey so far, offering encouragement for your future as a bread baker.

12.1 Reflecting on Your Progress

Think back to when you first started your bread-making journey. Whether this book was your first introduction to baking or you had a little experience under your belt, you've undoubtedly come a long way. You've learned how to mix, knead, and proof dough, and you've made everything from simple sandwich loaves to crusty artisan breads.

You've also tackled sourdough, experimented with high-hydration doughs, and explored the unique flavors and techniques behind breads from around the world. Along the way, you've likely faced challenges—maybe a loaf didn't rise as expected, or your dough was too sticky to handle—but you pushed through and gained valuable knowledge from each experience.

Every loaf you bake, every mistake you learn from, and every new recipe you try builds your skills and confidence. Bread making is both an art and a science, and with practice, you'll continue to refine your techniques and create better and more consistent results.

12.2 The Joy of Experimentation

As you grow more comfortable with bread making, one of the most exciting aspects is the freedom to experiment. Bread is a wonderfully forgiving medium for creativity. You can personalize each loaf to suit your tastes, explore new flavors, and develop your own signature breads.

Experiment with Flavors

- **Herbs and Spices**: Try adding different combinations of herbs and spices to your dough. Fresh rosemary in a rustic loaf, garlic and thyme in a focaccia, or cinnamon and cardamom in a sweet bread can completely transform the flavor.
- **Nuts and Seeds**: Play around with different textures by adding nuts and seeds to your dough or sprinkling them on top. Try

sunflower seeds in a multigrain loaf, or walnuts and dried cranberries in a hearty whole wheat bread.

- **Cheese and Savory Add-ins**: Experiment with folding in cheeses, roasted vegetables, or olives for savory loaves. A cheddar and jalapeño loaf, for example, makes a fantastic accompaniment to soups or stews.
- **Fruits and Sweet Add-ins**: For sweet breads, try adding dried fruits, chocolate chips, or even fresh berries. A cinnamon-raisin loaf or a chocolate babka can take your bread from a simple staple to a decadent treat.

Experiment with Techniques

- **Advanced Shaping**: Now that you've mastered basic loaf shapes, challenge yourself with more intricate designs. Try braiding challah, shaping baguettes, or creating decorative scoring patterns on your sourdough loaves.

- **Fermentation Times**: Play around with fermentation times to create deeper flavors. Experiment with longer, cooler rises for a tangier sourdough, or try refrigerating your dough overnight to see how it affects the crumb and flavor.
- **Alternative Grains**: Explore different types of flour, like rye, spelt, or einkorn, to see how they influence the taste and texture of your bread. Incorporating whole grains or ancient grains can also add nutritional value to your loaves.

12.3 Sharing Your Bread with Others

One of the greatest joys of bread making is sharing your creations with others. Bread is a universal food that brings people together, and there's something incredibly fulfilling about baking for friends, family, and even your community.

Give the Gift of Bread
Homemade bread makes a thoughtful and personal gift. Whether it's a rustic loaf of sourdough, a sweet brioche, or a batch of freshly baked rolls, your bread will be appreciated by anyone lucky enough to receive it. Consider baking bread as a gift for holidays, special occasions, or simply as a way to show appreciation to someone.

Host a Bread-Themed Gathering
If you enjoy baking bread, why not host a bread-themed dinner or gathering? You could serve a variety of breads with different accompaniments like cheeses, spreads, and soups. A bread board with different types of homemade loaves, served with flavored butters or olive oil, can be a fantastic centerpiece for a meal with friends.

Teach Others

Now that you have a solid foundation in bread making, consider passing on your knowledge to others. Whether it's teaching a family member, friend, or a local group, sharing your skills helps spread the joy of bread making. You might be surprised at how much you learn through teaching, and the satisfaction of seeing others enjoy the process is rewarding.

12.4 Sustainable Bread Making

As you continue your bread-making journey, consider how you can make your process more sustainable. Bread making offers numerous opportunities to reduce waste, support local ingredients, and create more environmentally friendly practices in the kitchen.

Reduce Food Waste

Leftover bread, stale loaves, or excess

dough doesn't need to be thrown away. There are countless ways to use up every bit of your bread:

- **Stale Bread** can be repurposed into breadcrumbs, croutons, bread pudding, or French toast.
- **Extra Dough** can be frozen for future use or turned into small rolls or flatbreads.

Use Local and Seasonal Ingredients

Whenever possible, use locally sourced ingredients to make your bread. Local flours, honey, fruits, and herbs not only support your community's economy but also add unique flavors to your creations. Experiment with seasonal ingredients like fresh herbs in the spring or roasted squash in the fall to highlight what's in season.

Consider Organic and Whole Grain Flours

Switching to organic or whole grain

flours can improve the nutritional content of your bread while supporting more sustainable farming practices. Whole grain flours add fiber, vitamins, and minerals to your loaves and offer a rich, nutty flavor that's often missing from refined white flours.

12.5 Continuing Your Bread-Making Education

Bread making is an art that you can continue to explore for years to come. There's always more to learn, whether it's perfecting a challenging technique, experimenting with new recipes, or diving deeper into the science behind fermentation and gluten development.

Explore Online Resources and Communities

There are countless resources online where you can find new recipes, tips, and advice from other bakers. Joining online bread-making communities can provide inspiration and troubleshooting support. Platforms like YouTube, Instagram, and specialized baking forums are filled with tutorials, masterclasses, and vibrant communities eager to share their knowledge.

Try New Bread Styles and Traditions

The world of bread is incredibly diverse, and there are still so many styles to explore. From Japanese milk bread (shokupan) to traditional Swedish rye bread (rågbröd), or Ethiopian injera, expanding your bread-making repertoire can take you on a cultural journey while honing your skills.

Experiment with Sourdough

If you haven't already, delve deeper into sourdough. The world of sourdough baking offers endless variations, from tangy boules to intricate sourdough croissants. Mastering sourdough fermentation allows you to work with wild yeast and bacteria, giving you full control over the flavor and texture of your bread.

12.6 The Reward of Homemade Bread

At the heart of bread making is the simple pleasure of creating something with your own hands. There's a meditative quality to working with dough, watching it rise, and savoring the transformation of simple ingredients into something delicious. The rewards go beyond just the physical loaf—it's the sense of accomplishment, the creative freedom, and the joy of sharing your work with others.

As you continue your journey, remember that each loaf is part of your growth as a baker. Embrace the process, learn from every bake, and most importantly, enjoy the bread you make. Whether you're a beginner or a seasoned baker, there's always something new to discover in the world of bread.

Conclusion: Keep Baking, Keep Exploring

Bread making is a journey that never truly ends. With every loaf, every experiment, and every shared slice, you're deepening your connection to this timeless craft. By now, you've built a solid foundation, and you have all the tools and knowledge you need to keep exploring, improving, and enjoying the process.

As you move forward, I encourage you to keep experimenting, share your love of bread with others, and most importantly—keep baking! The world of bread is as vast and varied as the people who bake it, and your journey is only just beginning..

If you enjoyed this title please leave a positive review.

Thank you..

Disclaimer *This eBook was created with the assistance of AI technology and is intended for informational purposes only. While every effort has been made to ensure the accuracy and usefulness of the content, it should not be considered professional or expert advice. Readers are encouraged to conduct their own research and consult with professionals where appropriate before making decisions based on the information provided in this eBook. The authors and publishers assume no responsibility or liability for any actions taken by readers based on the content of this eBook*